Meditating with MANDALAS

DAVID FONTANA

Turn the pages of this inspirational guide and explore the exciting world of mandalas! Learn step by step how to use mandalas as a visual aid for entering a meditative state, and make your own mandalas with the tools and materials in this kit. (See pages 24–31 to learn more about creating mandalas.)

Table of Contents

INTRODUCING MANDALAS 5

- THE MANDALA TRADITION 7
- MANDALAS AND MEDITATION 9
- STARTING MEDITATION 12
- WORKING WITH THIS BOOK 13
- STILLING BODY AND MIND 16
- HOW MANDALAS WORK 19
- WHAT MANDALAS REVEAL 22
- MAKING YOUR OWN MANDALA 24
- SYMBOLISM 27
- CONTINUING THE PRACTICE 29

MANDALAS FOR MEDITATION 33

- A CELTIC CROSS 34
- A SNOWFLAKE 36
- THE WHEEL OF TRUTH 38
- AN OCTOPUS 40
- FLOATING LOTUS 42
- SUN LOTUS 44
- NATURE'S HARMONY 46
- CRANES AMONG CLOUDS 48
- THE FLUTE PLAYER 50
- THE FLOWER OF SELF 52
- THE STAR IN THE WELL 54
- THE SALMON OF KNOWLEDGE 56
- JEWELS 58
- DOLPHINS AT PLAY 60
- A WATER GARDEN 62

CLOSING THOUGHTS 64

Introducing Mandalas

MANDALAS ARE SYMBOLIC PICTURES USED IN MEDITATION. IMPORTANT IN MOST EASTERN TRADITIONS, THEY TAKE THE MEDITATOR ON A WORDLESS JOURNEY INTO THE MIND'S DEEPEST MYSTERIES.

Mandalas are probably as old as humankind. In rudimentary form they appear in some of the earliest marks made by humans, and they are present again in some of the first scribbles of young children. They express through symbolism something innate in ourselves. Like all true symbols they arise from deep levels of the unconscious, and as such serve as keys which can take us into the mysterious recesses of our own minds.

The most basic of all mandalas is the circle, an intriguing symbol that has no beginning and no end and encloses a symmetrical area of space in such a way that each point on the circumference of that space is equidistant from the center. It is the still center of the turning world, the magic circle that defines and protects a sacred space within which one finds tranquillity and peace. It is

The circle of the mandala is a primal symbol for all that exists. It is the symbol of the sun, the giver of light, and of the full moon, the discloser of dark mysteries.

the wheel of life, the symbol of ultimate perfection, the tunnel between this world and the world to come, the symbol of eternity.

Not only is the circle the most basic of all mandalas, it is the form upon which all mandalas are based – the word "mandala" is in fact the Sanskrit word for "disk." Although the circle may contain other shapes within it, such as the square and the triangle, and sometimes may even be bounded on the outside by one or other of these shapes, the circle remains the primary feature of all mandalas. Without the circle, there is no mandala. But once the circle is drawn, then other symbols can be added to it. These more complex mandalas are major features of the sacred art of many spiritual traditions, particularly of Hinduism and Buddhism. At their most complete, these elaborate mandalas constitute symbolic pictures of the cosmos, replete either with the divine beings who represent or embody the cosmic forces behind existence, or with the geometrical shapes that signify these forces in more abstract form – the term "yantra" is sometimes used for these purely geometrical mandalas.

In the spiritual traditions, the mandala is frequently used as an aid to meditation. Because of its symbolic nature, when used in this way, the mandala can help the mind not only to become focused and tranquil, but also to access progressively deeper levels of the unconscious, ultimately assisting the meditator to experience a mystical sense of oneness with the ultimate unity from which the cosmos in all its manifold forms arises.

THE MANDALA TRADITION

Although mandalas are particularly associated with the East, they have in fact been an important feature of Western traditions as well. In Christianity one of the best-known examples is the Celtic Cross below, in which the center of the circle is also the center of the cross, whose four arms then extend beyond the circumference to symbolize, among other things, the four dimensions, the human form, and the link between the heavens above and the earth below. In fact, the symbol probably predates Christianity. We sometimes see the cross contained fully within the circle, while at other times it is much smaller and takes the form of the rose, as in the "rosy cross" of the Rosicrucians. There are also echoes of the mandala in the halo that surrounds the head of Christ and the saints in Christian art.

In Islam, which forbids the portrayal of Allah or of Muhammad, geometrical shapes dominate sacred art, and a segment of the circle,

the crescent, together with the full circle in the form of a star, represent the divine. The inverted half circle, the dome, represents the arch of the heavens and, by forming the roof of the mosque, allows the whole building to become a mandala, helping to turn the minds of the faithful toward Allah.

In Hinduism, Buddhism and Jainism, the three great traditions that originated in India, the mandala is an integral part of sacred art and a central feature of many meditational practices. The ground plan of the Hindu temple often takes the form of a mandala symbolizing the universe, with doors or gates at each of the cardinal points. Sometimes colors are associated with each of these points – yellow for the north, red for the east, black for the south and white for the west – while the center, the point at which all four meet and from which all four arise, is green, the color of creation. For the Jains and also for Hindus and Buddhists the lotus is sacred not only because its flower transcends the darkness of the water and of the mud where it has its roots, but also because its symmetrical petals make a perfect mandala. In Buddhism the mandala is an essential feature of the Tibetan tradition, in some of its more elaborate forms representing a mystical journey that takes the meditator from ignorance to enlightenment. In the West the circular maze, such as the one on the floor of Chartres Cathedral in northern France, is another representation of the symbolic journey from outer darkness to the sacred center of the spirit, where the individual soul finds itself in the presence of the divine.

MANDALAS AND MEDITATION

Meditation is a practice for calming the mind. Usually our minds are so dominated by what is going on around us or by our own mental chatter that we have little opportunity to experience the peaceful, tranquil state that is the natural condition of the mind. So habitual does this domination become that we take it for granted. If we are asked to stop thinking for one minute, most of us would be unable to do so. In a very real sense, our minds are not our own. They are so distracted first by one thing, then another, and so pulled this way and that by sensations, thoughts, memories and emotions and by the demands of the outer world that we have very little control over them. The result is that we live much of our waking lives in a state of tension; and when the mind becomes tense, so does the body. Mind and body are so closely linked that many of our physical ailments are a consequence, directly or indirectly, of what goes on inside our heads.

Meditation helps the mind to learn to become focused upon just one stimulus, and to cease to attend to all the distractions competing for our attention. The stimulus may be our breathing, or it may be a mantra (a sacred sound or phrase) or a mandala. If we use our breathing, we simply place our awareness upon the subtle sensation at the base of the nostrils as we breathe in and out. If we use a mantra, we repeat it over and over to ourselves. And if we choose a mandala, we place our gaze softly and attentively upon the image. In each case, whenever our thoughts begin to stray, we bring them gently but firmly back to the point of focus. We do not force ourselves to stop thinking. Thoughts will inevitably arise, particularly when we are beginning to learn meditation or when we have had a busy or fretful day, but when they do so we simply refrain from attending to them. They are there, but we take no particular notice of them and do not allow them to take control of our minds.

Why meditate?

Meditation is a path of self-discovery. We may think that we know ourselves, but in fact we live mostly in our conscious minds, and remain unaware of the depths of our unconscious and of the subtle spiritual dimension of our own being. By helping to still the train of thoughts that dominates the conscious mind, meditation opens us to the deeper mysteries of our inner selves.

The results of such a boost in mental power can be seen on an everyday level. By increasing our ability to concentrate, meditation can aid memory and make us more alert to the world around us. It also has potential physical benefits: it helps to relax the body and combat the effects of stress. There is evidence that for some people meditation may help to lower blood pressure, assist with pain management, and promote restful, restorative sleep. It may help to lift the spirits, and by relaxing the mind and body may even improve our physical appearance.

Because vision has always been such an important part of human experience, the mandala has proved over the centuries to be a particularly helpful point of focus in meditation. Whatever form it takes, it can often hold our attention more effectively than non-visual stimuli. A mandala also has the added advantage that, provided it is a true mandala, its symbolic content will take us, without our having to make any special effort, into that inner world that lies at the heart of meditation.

STARTING MEDITATION

When you begin meditating with mandalas, even if you have practiced meditation before, it is best to start with accessible designs, such as the ones contained in this book. The traditional, elaborate mandalas used in much of Tibetan Buddhism can and should be used only under detailed instructions from a lama who has himself been initiated into the spiritual practices that they represent. Use of these mandalas by the uninitiated is unlikely to do much good. The meditator can all too easily become distracted by the strength of the images and the vibrancy of the colors, and by the multitude of questions that they are likely to arouse in his or her mind. Like a secret code, to which the meditator does not have the key, the mandala will refuse to reveal its secrets. Instead, it is better to begin with something more simple, commencing if you wish with geometrical shapes.

Geometrical shapes have an archetypal force in that they are part of our inherited psyche, representing the patterns of the natural world within our minds. The mystery schools of ancient Greece, particularly that of Pythagoras, made a special study of geometry for this reason, and many of the sacred sites of the ancient world, such as the pyramids of Egypt and South America, and the stone circles of Western Europe, including Stonehenge, were constructed to conform to what is known as "sacred geometry," which reproduced through man-made objects the patterns upon which this world, the heavens and the cosmos itself were thought to have been constructed.

If you start with a mandala based on a geometrical shape such as a Celtic Cross (see page 34), you will find that early in your meditation a number of its symbolic meanings will arise unbidden in your mind. Without forcing it, simply allow this to happen. Note these meanings, without judgment, as they arise. Note how they seem to emerge of themselves from some deep level of your unconscious. But do not be tempted to linger over any one of them or to try to commit them to memory. You can ponder their significance after the meditation is over.

WORKING WITH THIS BOOK

Resist the temptation to flip through this book, glancing at one mandala after another without really taking them in. This doesn't mean that you must work with each of them before you can go on to the next. By all means look through the book – probably you will do so anyway – but keep in mind that you are not simply looking at pretty pictures. The mandalas are very much more than that. They each have a symbolic life of their own, and coming to know them will take time, just as it takes time to come to know new friends.

There are 15 mandalas for guided meditation in the book that you can work with in the order they are presented. But avoid thinking of the mandalas as forming a sequence from easy to difficult. Each mandala is complete in itself. There is no hierarchy between them. Some are based on traditional Tibetan mandalas while others are inspired by nature; others again are based on symbols found in various cultures, from Japan to Celtic Europe. When selecting a new mandala on which to meditate, you can do this on a purely visual basis, choosing the one that appeals to you most at that time. Alternatively, you might consider the mandalas' symbols: the step-by-step text alongside each mandala is ideal for anyone who feels daunted by the thought of approaching the images without specific guidance (see page 33).

Mandala meditation step by step

Meditation is at one and the same time disarmingly simple yet challengingly difficult. Simple because the basic principles are readily learned, but difficult because the mind stubbornly refuses to keep to them. The secret is patience and practice. Meditation cannot be learned in a few days. But if you remain patient with yourself and practice regularly, progress will come.

1 Find a quiet room where you won't be disturbed. Sit cross-legged on a firm cushion that raises your bottom a little way above the floor or sit in an upright chair with your feet flat on the floor – whichever you find most comfortable.

2 Place the mandala you have chosen at eye level about an arm's length, or slightly more, in front of you. Start with a basic pattern such as a Celtic Cross (see page 34). If using a mandala that is not in this book, make sure that it is at least the same size as a page of this book. Straighten your back and rest your hands in your lap, fingers laced together and palms uppermost.

3 Now rest your gaze on the mandala but relax your eye muscles. If your eyes go into soft focus so that you can see two images of the mandala instead of one, no matter. This is better than straining your eyes. Blink only as often as necessary. Remain focused on the image. Do not be distracted by any thoughts that arise. If your attention wanders, bring it back each time to the mandala. Try not to think about the mandala. Simply look at it, steadily and evenly.

To begin with, practice for five minutes each day. If before five minutes are up you begin to feel disturbed in any way by the visual nature of the experience (see page 23), draw the meditation to a close. Remain always within the time limit in which you feel comfortable. As you become used to this form of meditation, you can extend this time limit, until ultimately you may be sitting for a full 20 or 30 minutes at each session. But never try to rush things or to push yourself too hard.

STILLING BODY AND MIND

The essence of meditation is stillness. Unless you are following various practices of the Jain tradition (one of the great spiritual traditions of India), which are performed while standing, meditation involves sitting on a cushion or on a chair and attempting to still both your body and your mind. Movement of any kind, apart from the gentle rise and fall of your breathing, disrupts the flow of meditation. This does not mean that if you are a beginner you must sit like a statue for hours on end. To begin with, five minutes may be quite long enough. But for these five minutes, try as long as is possible to remain still. Almost immediately, you will find that the body wants you to move. The body is used to controlling you rather than being controlled by you, and it will begin to try and distract you with the urge to shift your position, to scratch your face, to slump forward, to ease some small discomfort or other. Resist these distractions, not by a fierce effort of will but by gently moving your attention away from them. They are there, but they are unimportant.

Consider, too, the movement of your eyes. Whenever we look at an image, we tend to scan it continually from one point of focus to another. If the image is an enigmatic one, we scan it even more, restlessly seeking information to explain it to ourselves. Notice yourself doing this when you begin to meditate with mandalas, and how difficult it is to keep your eyes

Experiencing stillness

Do not become bored with the mandala. We live in a world of constant, instant gratification. Watch a television program and notice how quickly each image changes, as if our attention span is so short that we cannot concentrate for more than a few seconds. Meditating on mandalas slows everything down. The frenetic pace of life becomes focused upon a still center. The mandala is the exact opposite of the flickering, ever-changing television screen.

When you start meditating with mandalas, the novelty of this unusual practice may hold your attention for the first few sessions, but then the restless mind may begin to cast around for new stimuli. Do not allow your mind to distract you. Return to mandala meditation. Remember that this restlessness is simply a result of modern living. The whole purpose of meditation is to free ourselves from this, and to experience the stillness that is our real nature.

still. However, this is not the way to meditate. Take in the whole of the image initially, but having done so allow your eyes to come to rest on one point. Usually this is the point just above the center, but there is no fixed rule about this. Do not strain your eyes. Allow them to slip into soft focus if you wish. Blink when you have to, but not more often than necessary. Notice how your eyes, as intent upon movement as your body, try to pull away from this point of focus in order to resume their scanning. Gently resist this attempt.

Just as the body is used to controlling you, so is the mind. Almost immediately you will find that thoughts start trying to intrude – thoughts about why you are meditating, about your daily life, about problems with work or with your relationships, about last summer's vacation or about next Christmas. As with bodily distractions, gently move your attention away from these thoughts. You cannot stop them arising, but you can stop them from dominating your awareness. Like the body, the mind is used to controlling you, and resents having to relinquish this control during the period of meditation. But you cannot meditate if you are distracted by thoughts rather than relaxing into stillness.

Similarly, let go of emotions. Anger or resentment at some remembered confrontation with colleagues, fear at the prospect of an impending challenge, sexual desires, happiness at the thought of a new relationship or of some future event, will all, like the body and the mind, try to distract you. Such emotions can emerge without you even realizing it, but they can dominate your mind as much as thoughts. Become aware of them, then let them go.

In order to remain undistracted by the body, by thoughts and by emotions, you need to keep refocusing your attention on the mandala. Vision is one of our strongest senses, and if the vision is held steadily upon an image, this helps to calm the restlessness of body, mind and emotions.

HOW MANDALAS WORK

Like all mandalas, the ones in this book are not artistic constructs, created to look colorful and attractive. Many successful visual artists, like successful poets and musicians, are open to a creative impulse that arises from deep levels of the unconscious. The artist expresses what is given to him or her, not what is put together by conscious thought. Ancient Greek sculptors, who produced some of the finest pieces in stone known to humankind, worked on the principle that hidden within the block of stone in front of them was the perfect form. Their task was simply to reveal it. If they allowed their own ideas, their own ego to intrude, then the finished piece was the work of man, not the work of the divine muses who inspired the creative spirit hidden within the stone. In the same way, the modern creative artist has to allow some inner impulse to take over from his or her own mind and express itself *through* the person, rather than *from* the person.

The mandalas in this book capture something of this artistic spirit. They are expressions of the deeper levels of consciousness that are common to us all. Thus when we contemplate them, they help us to access these deeper levels within ourselves. But do not expect too much of the mandalas. They cannot do the work of meditation for us. What they *can* do is provide us with the stimulus, a form of road map which, if we read it well, will guide us toward a level of understanding.

Looking at it like this, mandalas are both static and dynamic. Static in that they represent stillness, but dynamic in that implicit in that stillness there is the concept of movement – both from one feature of the mandala to another, and within the meditator. There is movement from the tensions of the body to a condition of physical relaxation; movement from the turmoil that is the habitual state of the mind to the tranquillity that is its real nature; and movement from the habitual superficial state of consciousness to something much deeper and wiser – movement in fact from the circumference of the circle into the heart that is its center.

We use mandalas by preventing our analytical mind, the mind that governs our waking life, from intruding between us and the visual experience of the mandala. We sit in meditation, with the mandala in front of us, and allow ourselves to take it into our visual space. It is as if this visual space, an expression of our consciousness, reaches out to embrace the mandala – or, if you prefer, as if we allow the visual space of the mandala to embrace our consciousness. Ultimately, there is no distinction between us and the mandala. It is outside ourselves, yet at the same time within the deepest recesses of our minds.

Becoming one with the mandala

In addition to shapes and colors, some mandalas – particularly those from the Tibetan Buddhist tradition – contain the figures of deities, such as the various Celestial buddhas. These beings are said to be personifications of the various energies that sustain creation and to exist both in their own right and as aspects of our own minds. Ultimately, it is said that there is no distinction between these energies and ourselves, for we are all aspects of the unity from which the world of appearances arises. Traditionally, the meditator seeks to experience the truth of this by incorporating the mandala into his or her own self – this is sometimes referred to as "awakening the mandala within oneself." Becoming one with the mandala in this way is a very advanced practice, undertaken only under the guidance of an experienced meditation teacher. However, even the inexperienced meditator may increasingly feel a sense of strong identification with the mandala, as if it expresses something profound about the self.

This is why in true meditation, it is important to come to a mandala without preconceptions about its meaning. Like any visual art, the mandala means what it is, not what we can put into words. If the mandala were a language of words, then it would be expressed in writing. Pictures and symbols communicate with a space within ourselves that is far deeper than words, far more basic and primal, and therefore far closer to the creative essence from which all things arise.

WHAT MANDALAS REVEAL

One way of approaching the mandala is as a wise friend who knows us even better than we know ourselves. If we have a wise friend, we do not interrupt him or her, we do not deny what our friend is telling us, we do not come between ourselves and the things that he or she is trying to convey. When you sit in meditation before your mandala, it is important to have the same attitude. The mandala will help you to meditate only if you allow it to do so.

A great Zen master once said to his pupil that the reason the pupil could not make progress was that he had "a too willful will." The pupil thought that he could not access the life-force within himself unless he "made it happen." The feeling that we must "make it happen" is endemic to our Western mind, ingrained in us by our education. The emphasis is always upon doing it for ourselves, upon learning for ourselves and assessing our own progress. This attitude is a great handicap in meditation.

Meditation is a process of opening our inner selves and allowing something to express itself that we did not know we possessed. Christianity puts it: "Be still and know that I am God." God, the Kingdom of Heaven, the life-force, the Divine spirit, call it what you will, is already within us. If it were not, we would not exist. Meditation is a process that allows the layer upon layer of conditioning acquired during our lives to be peeled away, so that this creative essence, the real expression of who we are, can reveal itself.

When you are meditating, contemplate the mandala and see what arises. However, if the sensations you are experiencing with a particular mandala disturb you, stop your meditation. The mandala you are working with may not be the right one for you at this time. Perhaps it is taking you too deep, too quickly. Perhaps it is unsuitable for your temperament. Sensitive spirits can sometimes be disturbed by a mandala that is too challenging or too abrupt. On the other hand, adventurous spirits may find that some mandalas are too neutral or too soporific. This is where a good meditation teacher can help: he or she can choose mandalas that are suited to your temperament. If you are working without a teacher, then this is an opportunity to look more closely at yourself. Notice to which mandalas you feel most drawn. Are you someone who seeks gentleness and calm, or an adventurous spirit who likes challenge, confrontation and change? You are who you are. No one temperament is better than another. Never force yourself into a category to which you do not belong. There will always be new mandalas that you can use. As you get used to this type of meditation, you may start to see mandalas in the world around you and elements of the world around you in mandalas.

MAKING YOUR OWN MANDALA

The great Swiss psychiatrist Carl Jung made an extensive study of mandalas, detecting in them a range of potential symbolic meanings. He noticed that as his clients progressed in the course of psychotherapy they spontaneously began to create their own mandalas. For Jung, mandalas were intimately associated with both psychological and spiritual health. When he built a house for himself at Bollingen, overlooking Lake Geneva, he constructed it in mandala form. You, too, will benefit from constructing your own mandalas.

When creating a mandala, there are certain guidelines to keep in mind. Firstly, it must not be the result of conscious effort. Rather than planning out

Using sand tubes and the mandala design sticker sheets

Peel off areas of the precut sheet you want to color. Sprinkle sand over the exposed sticky shapes, letting excess sand fall away.

Avoid preconceptions

Creating your own mandala is not a test of your progress in meditation and can be a meditative exercise in and of itself. Use the colored pencils in this kit and work on a sheet of paper of at least 8-½" x 11". Put yourself in a meditative frame of mind. Try to drop any preconceptions of how your mandala should look. Work freehand, as you can always carry out minor corrections later if you wish. Start with a geometrical shape, whichever one comes to mind, then add colors and other shapes as they come to mind. The whole process should be creative and spontaneous, arising from the unconscious rather than from conscious deliberation. Don't try for balance. Draw what comes. The results may surprise you.

If you are not satisfied with your mandala, put it aside, and perhaps try working with it again when the mood takes you.

a detailed composition, you should allow the design to emerge naturally. The mandala should arise from your unconscious, as if given to you by some power greater than yourself. It may be that your mandala will appear in your mind spontaneously during a meditation session. Or you may wish to sit before a blank sheet of paper, empty your mind of thoughts, and just draw whatever comes to mind. It may take several attempts before something arrives that seems to speak directly to you.

Secondly, the mandala is not simply a drawing inside a circle or square. It should have a recognizable symmetry and convey a sense of balance and harmony. It should represent something beyond its immediate appearance, something that you feel will reveal itself little by little as you meditate on it.

Thirdly, never try to force the pace. If something meaningful does not arise, no matter. Don't see this as failure. You may prefer to stay with the mandalas created by others. Traditional mandalas have stood the test of time, meaning that they represent something profound and enduring in ourselves.

Fourthly, don't be afraid to put your mandala to one side if you become dissatisfied with it. Don't allow yourself to become attached to it just because it's your own. It is simply there to help you, and if it ceases to do so, be prepared to let it go.

Instead of creating your own mandala, you may feel moved to adapt one of those in this book. Their purpose is to help you to experiment with meditation. But once again, be sure to work from your unconscious mind rather than from your normal, analytical consciousness. Don't be tempted to alter a mandala simply to make it look more attractive. Mandalas are things of beauty, but their beauty is an expression of their underlying meaning and harmony. They should never be seen simply as decorative objects. And don't be tempted to try altering one of the mandalas that come from the great spiritual traditions: they already have their own timeless wisdom.

SYMBOLISM

Carl Jung noted that the mandalas his patients produced tended to develop more harmony and meaning as their treatment progressed. In his view the center of the mandala can be seen as symbolizing the self, the total personality, while the periphery represents everything that belongs to the self – that is, the opposing elements that make up the total personality. For Jung, psychological health is always a matter of balancing these elements within oneself, so that the personality experiences an inner harmony and can express all its natural energies in an appropriate and effective way.

As you progress in meditation, you may find that the symbolism in the various mandalas with which you are working becomes increasingly apparent. Some symbols carry an almost universal meaning, while others are personal to yourself. As you meditate, do not make a particular attempt to identify symbolism in the mandala, or to speculate as to the meaning intended by the creator of the mandala. Symbols work best if they are received initially at an unconscious level and their meaning is allowed to arise spontaneously into conscious awareness. Nevertheless, some prior knowledge of symbols that carry universal meaning can be helpful to the more advanced meditator.

Shapes also carry symbolic meaning. The cross represents the descent of the divine life-force into matter. The circle symbolizes completion, movement, perfection, with no end and no beginning. The square stands for balance, safety and the four directions. The upward-pointing triangle symbolizes man's ascent to the divine, while the downward-pointing triangle represents the divine reaching down to man. Jung considered that the relationship between the circle and the square was of particular symbolic importance to the meditator. He referred frequently in his writings to "squaring the circle", which we can take to mean the act of reconciling the square, symbolizing consciousness and the outer material world, with the circle, symbolizing the unconscious and the inner spiritual world. Such reconciliation makes conscious the mysteries hidden within the unconscious.

The 15 mandalas in this book reflect the traditional symbolism of various cultures around the world – but with a degree of imaginative invention, too. Meditators are advised to follow the approaches I have described in this introduction. But initially you might like to acquaint yourself with some of the intuitive symbolic thinking behind these new mandalas, as described in

Color and Meaning

Buddhist mandalas traditionally use four basic colors - white, yellow, red and green - that represent the four directions, as well as the four elements of the human personality analogous to those identified by the psychologist Hans Eysenck (extroversion, introversion, stability and neuroticism). White also symbolizes purity, while yellow symbolizes the divine principle expressed in matter. Red represents energy and the life-force, and green the natural world. Subsequently, blue has been used to symbolize infinity and peace, while purple and violet both stand for mysticism and spiritual attainment.

Coloring your mandala

Be mindful of color associations, but choose colors intuitively as you fill in your mandala with the colored pencils in this kit.

the step-by-step guidelines accompanying each one. For advice on how to use these, see page 33.

CONTINUING THE PRACTICE

It is for you to decide how to continue with mandala meditation. You may wish to include it as part of another meditation program – for example, one that focuses upon breathing – and use it only from time to time.

Alternatively, you may choose to use mandala meditation as your main program. Either way, to make progress in meditation try to sit each day, either morning or evening or both, for at least 20 to 30 minutes. Build up to this slowly, never trying to force the pace. If possible, try to sit at the same time each day, and establish, if you can, a special place – such as the corner of a room – in which to sit, with a cushion or a chair that you use only for meditation. Wear something light and comfortable, such as pajamas or a robe, preferably in a tranquil color that will harmonize with the tranquillity of your meditation.

Seeking the truth

Dogen, the founder of the Soto Zen tradition, taught that one does not meditate in order to become a buddha, but because meditation is what buddhas do. In other words, the very act of sitting in meditation is the act of a buddha. Dogen is referring, of course, to genuine meditation, not simply to sitting lost in thought. But his teaching makes clear that meditation is not only for advanced practitioners. It belongs to us all, as it is the natural state of the mind when the mind becomes still. Meditation does not add something to the mind that is not already there. It strips away the obscurations that prevent the mind from experiencing its own true nature.

This profound truth is a great incentive to continue practicing. In meditation we are re-discovering insights into ourselves that have always been there but are now forgotten – also insights that not only confirm our humanity but that reveal that we are spiritual beings, expressions of the unifying creative force from which all things, both seen and unseen, arise.

If you have created your own mandala, use it if it feels right, but be ready to create a new mandala for yourself if you feel the urge. Notice how the new mandala differs from the old. Meditation is not a form of psychotherapy such as that used by Carl Jung with his patients, but nevertheless you may be aware of subtle developments in your mandala. Don't try to analyze these too closely, nor consciously to "improve" your mandala in an effort to demonstrate that you are making progress. However, note that these differences in shapes and colors may reflect a growing state of inner harmony and balance.

If after persevering with meditation for some time it seems to bring no benefits, don't be discouraged. Changes may have taken place at an unconscious level. And many meditators, although they may stop practicing at certain points in their lives, come back to it later. If you find that you have no wish to continue with meditation for the present, put this book to one side, but try not to forget it completely. Like everything to do with meditation, it is here to help you. To adapt the words of one of the greatest of all teachers (Jesus Christ), meditation is made for man and not man for meditation. It remains, like a wise and loyal friend, ever ready to come to our assistance when we need it, such as periods of stress or uncertainty, whenever we need to find the peace that lies always deep within ourselves.

Mandalas for Meditation

HOW TO USE THE GUIDELINES

The step-by-step guidelines alongside each meditation are intended to introduce the beginner to some of the thinking behind the image and to open the mind to some of its possible symbolic resonances. As your meditative practice develops, these guidelines can be left behind, so the mandalas are allowed to work at an increasingly more intuitive and personal symbolic level. Although the mandalas are organized theme by theme for ease of reference, your experience of any of the mandalas is very much your own, and the thematic structure should not be taken as definitive. All the mandalas are, at the deepest level, a reflection of the self, the cosmos and the love that binds everything together.

A Celtic Cross

The Celtic cross combines two powerful symbols: the circle, suggesting infinity or the eternal; and the cross, suggesting the world of physical forms. In ancient times the image probably denoted creativity.

If you want to understand the Creator,
seek to understand created things.
—*St Columbanus (c. 543—615)*

1

Look at the two basic forms: in essence, the circle suggests the feminine principle and the cross the masculine principle. The interplay of both is all creation.

2

Now move to a higher level of symbolism, seeing the circle as eternity and the cross as the created world. The arms of the cross represent the points of the compass and the four elements.

3

See the fifth element, spirit, as the circle, which also is the circle of life and the endless path of knowledge, all fused into an all-embracing cosmic harmony. Let this enter your mind like water filling a well.

A Snowflake

The snowflake is fleetingly beautiful: We scarcely have time to admire it before it melts. Such is the way of the world: Our lives, our loves, are endless change. But at the center is the unchanging spirit.

Weak overcomes strong,
soft overcomes hard.
—Tao Te Ching (4th or 3rd Century BC)

1

Look at the snowflake in this mandala, one of an infinite number of snowflakes, yet complete and perfect within itself. Observe its perfect symmetry, and be aware as you appreciate the design that no other snowflake in the entire cosmos is identical to this one. Let this thought sink into your mind. Spend a few minutes relishing this frequent miracle.

2

Consider the snowflake's intrinsic strength, which comes from its unique beauty. The snowflake is fleeting yet flawless.

3

Imagine that the snowflake is on the point of melting. You are observing it in the moment of its being, from the fleeting viewpoint of your own lifetime.

The Wheel of Truth

The wheel in this mandala, based on a Tibetan original, symbolizes the teachings of Buddhism, including the goals of absolute selflessness and true perception. Its central spirals denote wisdom and compassion.

Happiness is when what you think, what you say and what you do are in harmony.
—Mohandas K. Gandhi (1869—1948)

1

Look at the square frame in which the mandala sits — representing the solidity and density of the material world.

2

Now turn to the wheel itself. The hub is a double yin yang symbol, around which are circles showing the steps toward enlightenment. The wheel's eight spokes symbolize the Buddha's Eightfold Path: right speech, right action, right livelihood, right effort, right mindfulness, right concentration, right view and right thought.

3

Look at the stylized lotus designs on the rim of the wheel, reflecting the pure heart that is filled with love and wisdom. Absorb the wheel into yourself as a guide and commitment to purity and wholeness.

An Octopus

The octopus is a symbol of the unfolding of creation from its mystic center, as well as an example of otherness. This mandala combines these meanings to give us a sense of who we are and what life is.

The enlightened soul is open to wonder.
Every marvel of nature mirrors the miracle of being alive.

—Modern meditation from Lisbon

1

Look at the random spirals of the octopus's eight arms. They suggest the endless energies of life as it unfolds out of the mystic center of creation.

2

Now think of the octopus as a creature with its own brain and its own individual mental landscape — not a mind, but a kind of world-view nonetheless.

3

The octopus squirts a cloud of black ink around itself to confuse its enemies. But you are not its enemy. You co-exist with the octopus and wish it no harm. Indeed, you respect its vital essence and the validity of the life it leads. Its strange beauty is a precious aspect of your cosmos.

Floating Lotus

The beauty of the lotus is that it remains untouched by either the water or the mud that nourish it – suggesting our undefiled spirit. This mandala has an overhead viewpoint, like an aerial photograph.

Those who know the truth
are not equal to those who love the truth.

—*Confucius (551—479 BC)*

1

Look at the swirling waters of the created world — they have their own divine beauty, and so are enclosed within a flower-shaped pool surround.

2

Turn your gaze to the central, circular pool of water. As if by magic, it reflects the starry night above. This is an image of the awesome vastness of the cosmos.

3

Contemplate the lotus at the heart of the mandala, with its central yin yang symbol. The lotus denotes pure spirit, embracing the complementary opposites that exist in this world and the cosmos.

4

Lastly, let these various beauties — water, sky, stars, flower, and our own contradictory natures — harmonize in your mind and bring you peace.

Sun Lotus

The center of this mandala is a solar spiral from which the sun's rays radiate. This is placed within a lotus, which depicts beauty growing from mud just as the soul rises from confusion to enlightenment.

Without self-knowledge
we are sundials in the shade.

—Modern meditation from Rome

1

Look at the outside of the mandala, the circle, which suggests perfection. Then contemplate the lotus, a symbol of potential perfection, within that frame.

2

Now turn your attention to the heart of the mandala. The spiral here could represent the meditator's journey into the self — as well as the primal flow of energy that makes the world what it is.

3

Feel how you relate to these different elements: the perfection (outer circle) that you can find within yourself if your heart is pure; the flowering of spirituality from the soil of incarnation (lotus); the energy of the sun (spiral), which drives your earthly being.

4

Let these elements fuse together in your mind, as in the totality of the mandala. Find peaceful self-awareness in this thought.

Nature's Harmony

Concentric circles bring a spiritual purity to this mandala, based on the order of the cosmos with its beautiful life and earth forms. The lotus design on the outer circle emphasizes the spiritual dimension.

All things share the same breath — the beast, the tree, the man. The air shares its spirit with all the life it supports.

—Chief Seattle (1786—1866)

1

Look at the sky, with its heavenly bodies, in the corners of this mandala. Then progress through the outer frame of lotus motifs. You find yourself symbolically in the realm of the mountains and the clouds.

2

Pass through the next circle into the greenery of nature, where trees, plants, birds and insects abound. This is Eden, the natural paradise.

3

Finally, penetrate to the mystic center, which borrows from nature to express its divine creativity. Imagine the central circle as the cross-section of a shaft of light that drills into your deepest self to awaken the spirit.

Cranes among Clouds

In the Japanese tradition cranes are symbols of good fortune. Clouds suggest the chance events that temporarily cast shadows over our lives. This meditation combines these evocative symbols.

Fortune will call
at the smiling gate.

—Japanese proverb

1

Identify the main elements of the mandala — the cranes, the blue sky, the clouds that sometimes block flying cranes from our view.

2

Keeping the mandala in your field of vision, let the details dissolve in your mind and give way to a view of empty blue sky. Let this blank sky fill your mind.

3

Visualize clouds forming a random pattern across this sky. They float across your consciousness. Then visualize a loose flock of cranes flying across the vista, passing in and out of the clouds randomly. Each crane that appears brings blessings into your life. Some of the cranes fly right through the clouds — like a happy outcome emerging from risk. Give thanks for such good fortune.

The Flute Player

The flute player is an image used by the 13th-century Persian poet Rumi to symbolize our longing for union with the spirit. The flute yearns to join its source – the reed bed from which it was originally cut.

Pure soul, how long will you travel? You are the King's falcon. Fly back toward the Emperor's whistle!

—Jalil al–Din Rumi (1207—1273)

1

Look at the flute player playing at sunset. Behind him are the clumps of reeds from which the flute was cut. Imagine that the music, the flute and the player are all one, and all feeling the call of the divine.

2

Think of the flute player's music as a soundless expression of his unconscious mind — a flowering of the soul in its purity.

3

Look at the other forms of life in the mandala — the waterlilies and fishes. Think of these too as yearning for unity: all the cosmos is one.

The Flower of Self

This is a mandala in which to lose and find oneself.
It reflects flowering self-awareness, the eternal self in full bloom,
the unchanging essence at the core of all our repeated days,
months and years.

Truth is inside you.
To see it you must open the inner eye.
—*The Buddha (c. 563–483 BC)*

∴1∴

Visually, trace the green, wave-like shoots that surround the central flower. They are lines of energy, each a wave of becoming revealing a flower of being. The bees are in perpetual motion, their wings beating faster than the eye can see.

∴2∴

Now turn your attention to the central flower. Take its many-petalled radiance into your mind, where it rests as a still reflection of your many-petalled self, the flowering of being beyond becoming.

∴3∴

There are two bees on the petals of this flower, but you do not brush them away: you are happy to let them live their fleeting moments on the wonderful flower of the spirit — like our own lifetimes.

The Star in the Well

Looking deep into our selves we see our greatest riches – suggested by a star in a well. Like any star, it is untouchable but undeniable. It gives us everything and nothing. It is the object of all our questing.

As far as we can discern, the sole purpose of human existence is to kindle a light in the darkness of mere being.

—Julian of Norwich (1342—c. 1416)

1

Identify the different stages and planes of the mandala: the outer world of nature, the rings of bricks, the square base within that, and lastly the hollow drop of the well itself.

2

Contemplate the star that you can see reflected in the water of the well. It shines brightly despite the darkness and the distance.

3

Think of yourself as looking right into the innermost depths of your own spirit. The deeper you penetrate, the brighter you shine. Your star is unique and beautiful, and can never be extinguished.

The Salmon of Knowledge

Because of its amazing ability to cross oceans and find its way unerringly to its spawning grounds, the Celts associated the salmon with prophecy. Meditate on the salmon to come closer to your intuitive wisdom.

Let your hook be always cast. In the pool where you least expect it, there will be fish.

—Ovid (43 BC—AD 17)

1

You are in the branches of a tree looking down. Two salmon are swimming in a circular pool below you. You can see also the leaves of the surrounding trees and the pool's decorative surround. Little hazelnuts are floating on the water's surface: these too are symbolic of prophetic insight.

2

Think of the salmon as a living yin yang symbol: one is male, the other female. Acknowledge both the male and female sides within yourself, as together they give you the gift of insight.

3

Draw the whole image within yourself. Feel the depths of your intuition. All reason can do is count the fish and the hazelnuts and decorate the pool edge; intuition can penetrate the inner depths, where love and truth are to be found.

Jewels

Gems were objects of wonder to the ancients, divine forces conjuring light from dark earth. In Eastern thought, jewels signified spiritual illumination. This bejeweled mandala contains the yin yang symbol, too.

Knowing what is enough
is wealth.

—Tao Te Ching (4th or 3rd Century BC)

1

Look at the different jewels and their colors.
There are diamonds, denoting radiance and integrity;
rubies, denoting love and courage;
pearls, denoting intuition and feminine wisdom;
sapphires, denoting peace and harmony.

2

See the pattern of the jewels in their delicate settings as being symbolic of the radiant and intricate order of the universe, illuminated by the intensely beautiful light of the spirit.

3

Let your eyes rest on the yin yang symbol — the creative interplay of opposites at the heart of our existence. The spirit adorns and transcends the body, as the jewels adorn and transcend male and female, light and dark, action and feeling.

Dolphins at Play

The dolphin is playful and communicative. Instinctively it takes joy in each moment. Dolphin symbolism is combined here with imagery of the ocean, from which all life evolved.

Grace is a gravity
that has learned how to play.

—Modern meditation from Los Angeles

~:1:~

Look at the dolphins swimming in the center and the two dolphins performing acrobatics around them. Their ability to break free of their own element, the water, and dance in another, the air, suggests our own potential for liberation once we have embraced the power of the spirit.

~:2:~

Contemplate the circle that the two dolphins make in their dance of joy. The circle suggests both spiritual perfection and the endless cycle of life, rising and falling, coming and going, like the dolphins.

~:3:~

Think of the vastness of the ocean, and the infinite expanse of sky above it. Taking the mandala into your mind, absorb the harmony of the cosmos. Our lives are gleaming droplets of water within the shining ocean of being.

A Water Garden

A garden is the universal symbol of harmony in nature and of the human soul which, just like a garden, must be in harmony with itself in order to find peace.

You are an ocean of knowledge
hidden in a dew drop.

—*Jalil al–Din Rumi (1207—1273)*

∴1∴

The life-giving powers of the water, which plays endlessly through the fountain, give sustenance to the fish, just as love gives sustenance to the soul.

∴2∴

The paving around the pond is made up of uneven blocks, perfectly fitted together — a symbol of the work done by unconditional love and of love's tolerance of imperfections.

∴3∴

Notice that you cannot focus on all four of the trees that flourish outside of the garden at once, but that you can hold them at the edge of awareness, just as love can contain all things. Think of love as the soil, rain and roots of existence.

Closing Thoughts

Continue meditating with the mandalas in this book, creating your own mandalas for meditation, and seeking out new mandalas that suit your temperament. Remaining on the path of self-discovery will lead to greater peace and overall well-being.